SACRED CONGREGATION FOR THE DOCTRINE OF THE FAITH

INSTRUCTION
ON CERTAIN ASPECTS
OF THE
"THEOLOGY

First published 1984 by the
Incorporated Catholic Truth Society
38-40 Eccleston Square, London SW1V 1PD

ISBN 0 85183 601 1

Translation: Vatican Polyglot Press

Printed by Tee & Whiten (The Lincoln's Inn Press Ltd.), Standard House, Bonhill Street, London EC2A 4DA

INSTRUCTION ON CERTAIN ASPECTS OF THE "THEOLOGY OF LIBERATION"

Introduction

The Gospel of Jesus Christ is a message of freedom and a force for liberation. In recent years, this essential truth has become the object of reflection for theologians, with a new kind of attention which is itself full of promise.

Liberation is first and foremost liberation from the radical slavery of sin. Its end and its goal is the freedom of the children of God, which is the gift of grace. As a logical consequence, it calls for freedom from many different kinds of slavery in the cultural, economic, social and political spheres, all of which derive ultimately from sin, and so often prevent people from living in a manner befitting their dignity. To discern clearly what is fundamental to this issue and what is a by-product of it, is an indispensable condition for any theological reflection on liberation.

Faced with the urgency of certain problems, some are tempted to emphasize, unilaterally, the liberation from servitude of an earthly and temporal kind. They do so in such a way that they seem to put liberation from sin in second place, and so fail to give it the primary importance it is due. Thus, their very presentation of the problems is confused and ambiguous. Others, in an effort to learn more precisely what are the causes of the slavery which they want to end, make use of different concepts without sufficient critical caution. It is difficult, and perhaps impossible, to purify these borrowed concepts of an ideological inspiration which is incompatible with Christian faith and the ethical requirements which flow from it.

The Sacred Congregation for the Doctrine of the Faith does not intend to deal here with the vast theme of Christian freedom and liberation in its own right. This it intends to do in a subsequent document which will detail in a positive fashion the great richness of this theme for the doctrine and life of the Church.

The present Instruction has a much more limited and precise purpose: to draw the attention of pastors, theologians, and all the faithful to the deviations, and risks of deviation, damaging to the faith and to Christian living, that are brought about by certain forms of liberation theology which use, in an insufficiently critical manner, concepts borrowed from various currents of marxist thought.

This warning should in no way be interpreted as a disavowal of all those who want to respond generously and with an authentic evangelical spirit to the "preferential option for the poor". It should not at all serve as an excuse for those who maintain an attitude of neutrality and indifference in the face of the tragic and pressing problems of human misery and injustice. It is, on the contrary, dictated by the certitude that the serious ideological deviations which it points out tend inevitably to betray the cause of the poor. More than ever, it is important that numerous Christians, whose faith is clear and who are committed to live the Christian life in its fullness, become involved in the struggle for justice, freedom and human dignity because of their love for their disinherited, oppressed and persecuted brothers and sisters. More than ever, the Church intends to condemn abuses, injustices and attacks against freedom, wherever they occur and whoever commits them. She intends to struggle, by her own means, for the defense and advancement of the rights of mankind, especially of the poor.

I - An aspiration

1. The powerful and almost irresistable aspiration that people have for *liberation* constitutes one of the principal *signs of the times* which the Church has to examine and interpret in the light of the Gospel.[1] This major phenomenon of our time is universally widespread, though it takes on different forms and exists in different degrees according to the particular people involved. It is, above all, among those people who bear the burdens of misery and in the heart of the disinherited classes that this aspiration expresses itself with the greatest force.

2. This yearning shows the authentic, if obscure, perception of the dignity of the human person, created "in the image and likeness of God" (*Gen* 1:26-27), ridiculed and scorned in the midst of a variety of different oppressions: cultural, political, racial, social and economic, often in conjunction with one another.

3. In revealing to them their vocation as children of God, the Gospel has elicited in the hearts of mankind a demand and a positive will for a peaceful and just fraternal life in which everyone will find respect and the conditions for spiritual as well as material development. This requirement is no doubt at the very basis of the aspiration we are talking about here.

4. Consequently mankind will no longer passively submit to crushing poverty with its effects of death, disease and decline. He resents this misery as an intolerable violation of his native dignity.

[1] Cf. *Gaudium et spes*, n. 4.

Many factors, and among them certainly the leaven of the Gospel, have contributed to an awakening of the consciousness of the oppressed.

5. It is widely known, even in still illiterate sections of the world, that, thanks to the amazing advances in science and technology, mankind, still growing in numbers, is capable of assuring each human being the minimum of goods required by his dignity as a person.

6. The scandal of the shocking inequality between the rich and poor—whether between rich and poor countries, or between social classes in a single nation—is no longer tolerated. On one hand, people have attained an unheard of abundance which is given to waste, while on the other hand so many live in such poverty, deprived of the basic necessities, that one is hardly able even to count the victims of malnutrition.

7. The lack of equity and of a sense of solidarity in international transactions works to the advantage of the industrialized nations so that the gulf between the rich and the poor is ever widening. Hence derives the feeling of frustration among third world countries, and the accusations of exploitation and economic colonialism brought against the industrialized nations.

8. The memory of crimes of a certain type of colonialism and of its effects often aggravates these injuries and wounds.

9. The Apostolic See, in accord with the Second Vatican Council, and together with the Episcopal Conferences, has not ceased to denounce the scandal involved in the gigantic arms race which, in addition to the threat which it poses to peace, squanders amounts of money so large that even a fraction of it would be sufficient to respond to the needs of those people who want for the basic essentials of life.

II - Expressions of this aspiration

1. The yearning for justice and for the effective recognition of the dignity of every human being needs, like every deep aspiration, to be clarified and guided.

2. In effect, a discernment process is necessary which takes into account both the theoretical and the practical *manifestations* of this aspiration. For there are many political and social movements which present themselves as authentic spokesmen for the aspirations of the poor, and claim to be able, though by recourse to violent means, to bring about the radical changes which will put an end to the oppression and misery of people.

3. So the aspiration for justice often finds itself the captive of ideologies which hide or pervert its meaning, and which propose to people struggling for their liberation goals which are contrary to the true purpose of human life. They propose ways of action which imply the systematic recourse to violence, contrary to any ethic which is respectful of persons.

4. The interpretation of the *signs of the times in the light of the Gospel* requires, then, that we examine the meaning of this deep yearning of people for justice, but also that we study with critical discernment the theoretical and practical expressions which this aspiration has taken on.

III - Liberation, a Christian theme

1. Taken by itself, the desire for liberation finds a strong and fraternal echo in the heart and spirit of Christians.

2. Thus, in accord with this aspiration, the theological and pastoral movement known as "Liberation Theology" was born, first in the countries of Latin America which are marked by the

religious and cultural heritage of Christianity, and then in other countries of the third world, as well as in certain circles in the industrialized countries.

3. The expression, "Theology of Liberation", refers first of all to a special concern for the poor and the victims of oppression, which in turn begets a commitment to justice. Starting with this approach, we can distinguish several, often contradictory ways of understanding the Christian meaning of poverty and the type of commitment to justice which it requires. As with all movements of ideas, the "theologies of liberation" present diverse theological positions. Their doctrinal frontiers are badly defined.

4. The aspiration for *liberation,* as the term itself suggests, repeats a theme which is fundamental to the Old and New Testaments. In itself, the expression "theology of liberation" is a thoroughly valid term: it designates a theological reflection centered on the biblical theme of liberation and freedom, and on the urgency of its practical realization.

The meeting, then, of the aspiration for liberation and the theologies of liberation is not one of mere chance. The significance of this encounter between the two can be understood only in light of the specific message of Revelation, authentically interpreted by the Magisterium of the Church.[2]

IV - Biblical foundations

1. Thus a theology of liberation correctly understood constitutes an invitation to theologians to deepen certain essential biblical themes with a concern for the grave and urgent questions which the contemporary yearning for liberation, and those movements which more or less faithfully echo it, pose for the Church.

[2] Cf. *Dei Verbum,* n. 10.

We dare not forget for a single instant the situations of acute distress which issue such a dramatic call to theologians.

2. The radical experience of *Christian liberty*[3] is our first point of reference. Christ, our Liberator, has freed us from sin and from slavery to the Law and to the flesh, which is the mark of the condition of sinful mankind. Thus it is the new life of grace, fruit of justification, which makes us free. This means that the most radical form of slavery is slavery to sin. Other forms of slavery find their deepest root in slavery to sin. That is why freedom in the full Christian sense, characterized by the life in the Spirit, cannot be confused with a licence to give in to the desires of the flesh. Freedom is a new life in love.

3. The "theologies of liberation" make wide use of readings from the book of Exodus. The exodus, in fact, is the fundamental event in the formation of the chosen people. It represents freedom from foreign domination and from slavery. One will note that the specific significance of the event comes from its purpose, for this liberation is ordered to the foundation of the people of God and the Covenant cult celebrated on Mt. Sinai.[4] That is why the liberation of the Exodus cannot be reduced to a liberation which is principally or exclusively political in nature. Moreover, it is significant that the term *freedom* is often replaced in Scripture by the very closely related term, *redemption*.

4. The foundational episode of the *Exodus* will never be effaced from the memory of Israel. Reference is made to it when, after the destruction of Jerusalem and the exile to Babylon, the Jewish people lived in the hope of a new liberation and, beyond that, awaited a definitive liberation. In this experience God is recognized as the Liberator. He will enter into a new Covenant

[3] Cf. *Ga* 5, 1 ff.
[4] Cf. *Ex* 24.

with His people. It will be marked by the gift of His Spirit and the conversion of hearts.[5]

5. The anxieties and multiple sufferings sustained by those who are faithful to the God of the Covenant provide the theme of several Psalms: laments, appeals for help and thanksgivings all make mention of religious salvation and liberation. In this context, suffering is not purely and simply equated with the social condition of poverty or with the condition of the one who is undergoing political oppression. It also includes the hostility of one's enemies, injustice, failure and death. The Psalms call us back to an essential religious experience: it is from God alone that one can expect salvation and healing. God, and not man, has the power to change the situations of suffering. Thus the "poor of the Lord" live in a total and confident reliance upon the loving providence of God.[6] Moreover, throughout the whole crossing of the desert, the Lord did not fail to provide for the spiritual liberation and purification of his people.

6. In the Old Testament, the prophets after Amos keep affirming with particular vigor the requirements of justice and solidarity and the need to pronounce a very severe judgment on the rich who oppress the poor. They come to the defense of the widow and the orphan. They threaten the powerful: the accumulation of evils can only lead to terrible punishments.

Faithfulness to the Covenant cannot be conceived of without the practice of justice. Justice as regards God and justice as regards mankind are inseparable. God is the defender and the liberator of the poor.

7. These requirements are found once again in the New Testament. They are even more radicalized as can be shown in the

[5] Cf. *Jr* 31, 31-34; *Ez* 36, 26 ff.
[6] Cf. *Ze* 3, 12 ff.

discourse on the *Beatitudes*. Conversion and renewal have to occur in the depths of the heart.

8. Already proclaimed in the Old Testament, the commandment of fraternal love extended to all mankind thus provides the supreme rule of social life.[7] There are no discriminations or limitations which can counter the recognition of everyone as *neighbour*.[8]

9. Poverty for the sake of the kingdom is praised. And in the figure of the poor, we are led to recognize the mysterious presence of the Son of Man who became poor himself for love of us.[9] This is the foundation of the inexhaustible words of Jesus on the judgment in *Mt* 25:31-46. Our Lord is one with all in distress; every distress is marked by his presence.

10. At the same time, the requirements of justice and mercy, already proclaimed in the Old Testament, are deepened to assume a new significance in the New Testament. Those who suffer or who are persecuted are identified with Christ.[10] The perfection that Jesus demands of His disciples (*Mt* 5:18) consists in the obligation to be merciful "as your heavenly Father is merciful" (*Lk* 6:36).

11. It is in light of the Christian vocation to fraternal love and mercy that the rich are severely reminded of their duty.[11] St. Paul, faced with the disorders of the Church of Corinth, forcefully emphasizes the bond which exists between participation in the sacrament of love and sharing with the brother in need.[12]

12. New Testament revelation teaches us that sin is the greatest evil, since it strikes man in the heart of his personality.

[7] Cf. *Dt* 10, 18-19.
[8] Cf. *Lc* 10, 25-37.
[9] Cf. *2 Co* 8, 9.
[10] Cf. *Mt* 25, 31-46; *Ac* 9, 4-5; *Col* 1, 24.
[11] Cf. *Jm* 5, ff.
[12] Cf. *1 Co* 11, 17-34.

The first liberation, to which all others must make reference, is that from sin.

13. Unquestionably, it is to stress the radical character of the delivrance brought by Christ and offered to all, be they politically free or slaves, that the New Testament does not require some change in the political or social condition as a prerequisite for entrance into this freedom. However, the *Letter to Philemon* shows that the new freedom procured by the grace of Christ should necessarily have effects on the social level.

14. Consequently, the full ambit of sin, whose first effect is to introduce disorder into the relationship between God and man, cannot be restricted to "social sin". The truth is that only a correct doctrine of sin will permit us to insist on the gravity of its social effects.

15. Nor can one localize evil principally or uniquely in bad social, political or economic "structures" as though all other evils came from them so that the creation of the "new man" would depend on the establishment of different economic and socio-political structures. To be sure, there are structures which are evil and which cause evil and which we must have the courage to change. Structures, whether they are good or bad, are the result of man's actions and so are consequences more than causes. The root of evil, then, lies in free and responsible persons who have to be converted by the grace of Jesus Christ in order to live and act as new creatures in the love of neighbour and in the effective search for justice, self-control and the exercise of virtue.[13]

To demand first of all a radical revolution in social relations and then to criticize the search for personal perfection is to set out on a road which leads to the denial of the meaning of the person and his transcendance, and to destroy ethics and its founda-

[13] Cf. *Jm* 2, 14-26.

tion which is the absolute character of the distinction between good and evil. Moreover, since charity is the principle of authentic perfection, that perfection cannot be conceived without an openness to others and a spirit of service.

V - The voice of the Magisterium

1. In order to answer the challenge levelled at our times by oppression and hunger, the Church's Magisterium has frequently expressed her desire to awaken Christian consciences to a sense of justice, social responsibility and solidarity with the poor and the oppressed, and to highlight the present urgency of the doctrine and imperatives contained in Revelation.

2. We would like to mention some of these interventions here: the papal documents *Mater et magistra, Pacem in terris, Populorum progressio,* and *Evangelii nuntiandi.* We should likewise mention the letter to Cardinal Roy, *Octogesima adveniens.*

3. The Second Vatican Council in turn confronted the questions of justice and liberty in the Pastoral Constitution, *Gaudium et spes.*

4. On a number of occasions, the Holy Father has emphasized these themes, in particular in the encyclicals *Redemptor hominis, Dives in misericordia,* and *Laborem exercens.* These numerous addresses recall the doctrine of the rights of man and touch directly on the problems of the liberation of the human person in the face of the diverse kinds of oppression of which he is the victim. It is especially important to mention in this connection the Address given before the 26th General Assembly of the United Nations in New York, October 2, 1979.[14] On January 28

[14] Cf. *AAS* 71 (1979) pp. 1144-1160.

of that same year, while opening the Third Conference of CELAM in Puebla, John Paul II affirmed that the complete truth about man is the basis for any real liberation.[15] This text is a document which bears directly upon the theology of liberation.

5. Twice the *Synod of Bishops* treated subjects which are directly related to a Christian conception of liberation: in 1971, justice in the world, and in 1974, the relationship between freedom from oppression and full freedom, or the salvation of mankind. The work of the Synods of 1971 and 1974 led Paul VI in his Apostolic Constitution *Evangelii nuntiandi* to clarify the connection between evangelization and human liberation or advancement.[16]

6. The concern for the Church for liberation and for human advancement was also expressed in the establishment of the Pon tifical Commission, *Justice and Peace.*

7. Numerous national Episcopal Conferences have joined the Holy See in recalling the urgency of authentic human liberation and the routes by which to achieve it. In this context, special mention should be made of the documents of the General Conferences of the Latin American episcopate at Medellin in 1968 and at Puebla in 1979.

Paul VI was present at the Medellin Conference and John Paul II was at Puebla. Both dealt with the themes of conversion and liberation.

8. Following Paul VI, who had insisted on the distinctive character of the Gospel message,[17] a character which is of divine origin, John Paul II, in his address at Puebla, recalled the three pillars upon which any authentic theology of liberation will rest: *truth about Jesus Christ, truth about the Church, and truth about mankind.*[18]

[15] Cf. *AAS* 71 (1979) p. 196.
[16] Cf. *Evangelii nuntiandi,* n. 25-33, *AAS* 68 (1976) pp. 23-28.
[17] Cf. *Evangelii nuntiandi,* n. 32, *AAS* 68 (1976) p. 27.
[18] Cf. *AAS* 71 (1979) pp. 188-196.

VI - A NEW INTERPRETATION OF CHRISTIANITY

1. It is impossible to overlook the immense amount of selfless work done by Christians, pastors, priests, religious or laypersons, who, driven by a love for their brothers and sisters living in inhuman conditions, have endeavored to bring help and comfort to countless people in the distress brought about by poverty. Among these, some have tried to find the most effective means to put a quick end to the intolerable situation.

2. The zeal and the compassion which should dwell in the hearts of all pastors nevertheless run the risk of being led astray and diverted to works which are just as damaging to man and his dignity as is the poverty which is being fought, if one is not sufficiently attentive to certain temptations.

3. The feeling of anguish at the urgency of the problems cannot make us lose sight of what is essential nor forget the reply of Jesus to the Tempter: "It is not on bread alone that man lives, but on every word that comes from the mouth of God" (*Mt* 4:4; cf. *Dt* 8:3).

Faced with the urgency of sharing bread, some are tempted to put evangelization into parentheses, as it were, and postpone it until tomorrow: first the bread, than the Word of the Lord. It is a fatal error to separate these two and even worse to oppose the one to the other. In fact, the Christian perspective naturally shows they have a great deal to do with one another.[19]

4. To some it even seems that the necessary struggle for human justice and freedom in the economic and political sense constitutes the whole essence of salvation. For them, the Gospel is reduced to a purely earthly gospel.

5. The different theologies of liberation are situated between the *preferential option for the poor,* forcefully reaffirmed without

[19] Cf. *Gaudium et spes,* n. 39; PIUS XI, *Quadragesimo anno: AAS* 23 (1931) p. 207.

ambiguity after Medellin at the Conference of *Puebla*[20] on the one hand, and the temptation to reduce the Gospel to an earthly gospel on the other.

6. We should recall that the preferential option described at *Puebla* is two-fold: for the poor and *for the young.*[21] It is significant that the option for the young has in general been passed over in total silence.

7. We noted above (cf. 3) that an authentic theology of liberation will be one which is rooted in the Word of God, correctly interpreted.

8. But from a descriptive standpoint, it helps to speak of *theologies* of liberation, since the expression embraces a number of theological positions, or even sometimes ideological ones, which are not simply different but more often incompatible with one another.

9. In this present document, we will only be discussing developments of that current of thought which, under the name "theology of liberation", proposes a novel interpretation of both the content of faith and of Christian existence which seriously departs from the faith of the Church and, in fact, actually constitutes a practical negation.

10. Concepts uncritically borrowed from marxist ideology and recourse to theses of a biblical hermeneutic marked by rationalism are at the basis of the new interpretation which is corrupting whatever was authentic in the generous initial commitment on behalf of the poor.

[20] Cf. n. 1134-1165 and n. 1166-1205.
[21] Cf. *Doc. de Puebla,* IV, 2.

VII - Marxist analysis

1. Impatience and a desire for results has led certain Christians, despairing of every other method, to turn to what they call "marxist analysis".

2. Their reasoning is this: an intolerable and explosive situation requires *effective action* which cannot be put off. Effective action presupposes a *scientific analysis* of the structural causes of poverty. Marxism now provides us with the means to make such an analysis, they say. Then one simply has to apply the analysis to the third-world situation, especially in Latin America.

3. It is clear that scientific knowledge of the situation and of the possible strategies for the transformation of society is a presupposition for any plan capable of attaining the ends proposed. It is also a proof of the seriousness of the effort.

4. But the term "scientific" exerts an almost mythical fascination even though everything called "scientific" is not necessarily scientific at all. That is why the borrowing of a method of approach to reality should be preceded by a careful epistemological critique. This preliminary critical study is missing from more than one "theology of liberation".

5. In the human and social sciences it is well to be aware above all of the plurality of methods and viewpoints, each of which reveals only one aspect of reality which is so complex that it defies simple and univocal explanation.

6. In the case of marxism, in the particular sense given to it in in this context, a preliminary critique is all the more necessary since the thought of Marx is such a global vision of reality that all data received from observation and analysis are brought together in a philosophical and ideological structure, which predetermines the significance and importance to be attached to them.

The ideological principles come prior to the study of the social reality and are presupposed in it. Thus no separation of the parts of this epistemologically unique complex is possible. If one tries to take only one part, say, the analysis, one ends up having to accept the entire ideology. That is why it is not uncommon for the ideological aspects to be predominant among the things which the "theologians of liberation" borrow from marxist authors.

7. The warning of Paul VI remains fully valid today: marxism as it is actually lived out poses many distinct aspects and questions for Christians to reflect upon and act on. However, it would be "illusory and dangerous to ignore the intimate bond which radically unites them, and to accept elements of the marxist analysis without recognizing its connections with the ideology, or to enter into the practice of class-struggle and of its marxist interpretation while failing to see the kind of totalitarian society to which this process slowly leads".[22]

8. It is true that marxist thought ever since its origins, and even more so lately, has become divided and has given birth to various currents which diverge significantly from one another. To the extent that they remain fully marxist, these currents continue to be based on certain fundamental tenets which are not compatible with the Christian conception of humanity and society. In this context, certain formulas are not neutral, but keep the meaning they had in the original marxist doctrine. This is the case with the "class-struggle". This expression remains pregnant with the interpretation that Marx gave it, so it cannot be taken as the equivalent of "severe social conflict", in an empirical sense. Those who use similar formulas, while claiming to keep only certain elements of the marxist analysis and yet to reject this analysis taken as a whole, maintain at the very least a serious confusion in the minds of their readers.

[22] Paul VI, *Octogesima Adveniens,* n. 34, *AAS* 63 (1971) pp. 424-425.

9. Let us recall the fact that atheism and the denial of the human person, his liberty and his rights, are at the core of the marxist theory. This theory, then, contains errors which directly threaten the truths of the faith regarding the eternal destiny of individual persons. Moreover, to attempt to integrate into theology an analysis whose criterion of interpretation depends on this atheistic conception is to involve oneself in terrible contradictions. What is more, this misunderstanding of the spiritual nature of the person leads to a total subordination of the person to the collectivity, and thus to the denial of the principles of a social and political life which is in keeping with human dignity.

10. A critical examination of the analytical methods borrowed from other disciplines must be carried out in a special way by theologians. It is the light of faith which provides theology with its principles. That is why the use of philosophical positions or of human sciences by the theologian has a value which might be called instrumental, but yet must undergo a critical study from a theological perspective. In other words, the ultimate and decisive criterion for truth can only be a criterion which is itself theological. It is only in the light of faith, and what faith teaches us about the truth of man and the ultimate meaning of his destiny, that one can judge the validity or degree of validity of what other disciplines propose, often rather conjecturally, as being the truth about man, his history and his destiny.

11. When modes of interpretation are applied to the economic, social and political reality of today, which are themselves borrowed from marxist thought, they can give the initial impression of a certain plausibility, to the degree that the present-day situation in certain countries is similar to what Marx described and interpreted in the middle of the last century. On the basis of these similarities, certain simplifications are made which, abstracting from specific essential factors, prevent any really rigorous examination of the causes of poverty and prolong the confusion.

12. In certain parts of Latin America, the seizure of the vast majority of the wealth by an oligarchy of owners bereft of social consciousness, the practical absence or the shortcomings of a rule of law, military dictators making a mockery of elementary human rights, the corruption of certain powerful officials, the savage practices of some foreign capital interests constitute factors which nourish a passion for revolt among those who thus consider themselves the powerless victims of a new colonialism in the technological, financial, monetary or economic order. The recognition of injustice is accompanied by a *pathos* which borrows its language from marxism, wrongly presented as though it were scientific language.

13. The first condition for any analysis is a total openness to the reality to be described. That is why a critical consciousness has to accompany the use of any working hypotheses that are being adopted. One has to realize that these hypotheses correspond to a particular viewpoint which will inevitably highlight certain aspects of the reality while leaving others in the shade. This limitation which derives from the nature of human science is ignored by those who, under the guise of hypotheses recognized as such, have recourse to such an all-embracing conception of reality as the thought of Karl Marx.

VIII - Subversion of the meaning of truth and violence

1. This all-embracing conception thus imposes its logic and leads the "theologies of liberation" to accept a series of positions which are incompatible with the Christian vision of humanity. In fact, the ideological core borrowed from marxism, which we are referring to, exercises the function of a *determining principle.* It has this role in virtue of its being described as "*scientific*", that is to say, true of necessity.

In this core, we can distinguish several components.

2. According to the logic of marxist thought, the "analysis" is inseparable from the *praxis,* and from the conception of history to which this *praxis* is linked. The analysis is for the marxist an instrument of criticism, and criticism is only one stage in the revolutionary struggle. This struggle is that of the proletarian class, invested with its mission in history.

3. Consequently, for the marxist, only those who engage in the struggle can work out the analysis correctly.

4. The only true consciousness, then, is the *partisan* consciousness.

It is clear that the concept of *truth* itself is in question here, and it is totally subverted: there is no truth, they pretend, except in and through the partisan praxis.

5. For the marxist, the *praxis,* and the truth that comes from it, are partisan *praxis* and truth because the fundamental structure of history is characterized by *class-struggle.* There follows, then, the objective necessity to enter into the class struggle, which is the dialectical opposite of the relationship of exploitation, which is being condemned. For the marxist, the truth is a truth of class: there is no truth but the truth in the struggle of the revolutionary class.

6. The fundamental law of history, which is the law of the class struggle, implies that society is founded on violence. To the violence which constitutes the relationship of the domination of the rich over the poor, there corresponds the counter-violence of the revolution, by means of which this domination will be reversed.

7. The class struggle is presented as an objective, necessary law. Upon entering this process on behalf of the oppressed, one "makes" truth, one acts "scientifically". Consequently, the conception of the truth goes hand in hand with the affirmation of necessary violence, and so, of a political amorality. Within this perspective, any reference to ethical requirements calling for courageous and radical istitutional and structural reforms makes no sense.

8. The fundamental law of class struggle has a global and universal character. It is reflected in all the spheres of existence: religious, ethical, cultural and institutional. As far as this law is concerned, none of these spheres is autonomous. In each of them this law constitutes the determining element.

9. In particular, the very nature of ethics is radically called into question because of the borrowing of these theses from marxism. In fact, it is the transcendent character of the distinction between good and evil, the principle of morality, which is implicitly denied in the perspective of the class struggle.

IX - The theological application of this core

1. The positions here in question are often brought out explicitly in certain of the writings of "theologians of liberation". In others, they follow logically from their premises. In addition, they are presupposed in certain liturgical practices, as for example a "Eucharist" transformed into a celebration of the people in struggle, even though the persons who participate in these practices may not be fully conscious of it. We are facing, therefore, a real system, even if some hesitate to follow the logic to its conclusion. As such, this system is a perversion of the Christian message as God entrusted it to His Church. This message in its entirety finds itself then called into question by the "theologies of liberation".

2. It is not the *fact* of social stratification with all its inequity and injustice, but the *theory* of class struggle as the fundamental law of history which has been accepted by these "theologies of liberation" as a principle. The conclusion is drawn that the class struggle thus undestood divides the Church herself, and that in light of this struggle even ecclesial realities must be judged.

The claim is even made that it would maintaining an illusion with bad faith to propose that love in its universality can conquer what is the primary structural law of capitalism.

3. According to this conception, the class struggle is the driving force of history. History thus becomes a central notion. It will be affirmed that God Himself makes history. It will be added that there is only one history, one in which the distinction between the history of salvation and profane history is no longer necessary. To maintain the distinction would be to fall into "dualism". Affirmations such as these reflect historicist immanentism. Thus there is a tendency to identify the kingdom of God and its growth with the human liberation movement, and to make history itself the subject of its own development, as a process of the self-redemption of man by means of the class struggle.

This identification is in opposition to the faith of the Church as it has been reaffirmed by the Second Vatican Council.[23]

4. Along these lines, some go so far as to identify God Himself with history and to define faith as "fidelity to history", which means adhering to a political policy which is suited to the growth of humanity, conceived of as a purely temporal messianism.

5. As a consequence, faith, hope and charity are given a new content: they become "fidelity to history", "confidence in the future", and "option for the poor". This is tantamount to saying they have been emptied of their theological reality.

6. A radical politicization of faith's affirmations and of theological judgments follows inevitably from this new conception. The question no longer has to do with simply drawing attention to the consequences and political implications of the truths of faith, which are respected beforehand for their transcendant value. In this new system, every affirmation of faith or of theology is

[23] Cf. *Lumen gentium,* n. 9-17.

subordinated to a political criterion. which in turn depends on the class struggle, the driving force of history.

7. As a result, participation in the class struggle is presented as a requirement of charity itself. The desire to love everyone here and now, despite his class, and to go out to meet him with the non-violent means of dialogue and persuasion, is denounced as counterproductive and opposed to love.

If one holds that a person should not be the object of hate, it is claimed nevertheless that, if he belongs to the objective class of the rich, he is *primarily* a class enemy to be fought. Thus the universality of love of neighbour and brotherhood become an eschatological principle, which will only have meaning for the "new man" who arises out of the victorious revolution.

8. As far as the Church is concerned, this system would see her *only* as a reality interior to history, herself subject to those laws which are supposed to govern the development of history in its immanence. The Church, the gift of God and mystery of faith, is emptied of any specific reality by this reductionism. At the same time, it is disputed that the participation of Christians who belong to opposing classes at the same Eucharistic Table still makes any sense.

9. In its positive meaning the *Church of the poor* signifies the preference given to the poor, without exclusion, whatever the form of their poverty, because they are preferred by God. The expression also refers to the Church of our time, as communion and institution and on the part of her members, becoming more fully conscious of the requirement of evangelical poverty.

10. But the "theologies of liberation", which reserve credit for restoring to a place of honor the great texts of the prophets and of the Gospel in defense of the poor, go on to a disastrous confusion between the *poor* of the Scripture and the *proletariat* of Marx. In this way they pervert the Christian meaning of the poor, and

they transform the fight for the rights of the poor into a class fight within the ideological perspective of the class struggle. For them, the *Church of the poor* signifies the Church of the class which has become aware of the requirements of the revolutionary struggle as a step toward liberation and which celebrates this liberation in its liturgy.

11. A further remark regarding the expression, *Church of the People,* will not be out of place here. From the pastoral point of view, this expression might mean the favored recipients of evangelization to whom, because of their condition, the Church extends her pastoral love first of all. On might also refer to the Church as people of God, that is, people of the New Covenant established in Christ.[24]

12. But the "theologies of liberation" of which we are speaking, mean by *Church of the People* a Church of the class, a Church of the oppressed people whom it is necessary to "conscientize" in the light of the organized struggle for freedom. For some, the people, thus understood, even become the object of faith.

13. Building on such a conception of the Church of the People, a critique of the very structures of the Church is developed. It is not simply the case of fraternal correction of pastors of the Church whose behavior does not reflect the evangelical spirit of service and is linked to old-fashioned signs of authority which scandalize the poor. It has to do with a challenge to the *sacramental and hierarchical structure* of the Church, which was willed by the Lord Himself. There is a denunciation of members of the hierarchy and the magisterium as objective representatives of the ruling class which has to be opposed. Theologically, this position means that ministers take their origin from the people who therefore designate ministers of their own choice in accord with the needs of their historic revolutionary mission.

[24] Cf. *Gaudium et spes,* n. 39.

X - A NEW HERMENEUTIC

1. The partisan conception of truth, which can be seen in the revolutionary *praxis* of the class, corroborates this position. Theologians who do not share the theses of the "theology of liberation", the hierarchy, and especially the Roman Magisterium are thus discredited *in advance* as belonging to the class of the oppressors. Their theology is a theology of class. Arguments and teachings thus do not have to be examined in themselves since they are only reflections of class interests. Thus, the instruction of others is decreed to be, in principle, false.

2. Here is where the global and all-embracing character of the theology of liberation appears. As a result, it must be criticized not just on the basis of this or that affirmation, but on the basis of its classist viewpoint, which it has adopted *a priori,* and which has come to function in it as a determining principle.

3. Because of this classist presupposition, it becomes very difficult, not to say impossible, to engage in a real dialogue with some "theologians of liberation" in such a way that the other participant is listened to, and his arguments are discussed with objectivity and attention. For these theologians start out with the idea, more or less consciously, that the viewpoint of the oppressed and revolutionary class, which is their own, is the single true point of view. Theological criteria for truth are thus relativized and subordinated to the imperatives of the class struggle. In this perspective, *orthodoxy* or the right rule of faith, is substituted by the notion of *orthopraxy* as the criterion of the truth. In this connection it is important not to confuse practical orientation, which is proper to traditional theology in the same way that speculative orientation is, with the recognized and privileged priority given to a certain type of *praxis.* For them, this praxis is the revolutionary *praxis* which thus becomes the supreme criterion for theological

truth. A healthy theological method no doubt will always take the *praxis* of the Church into account and will find there one of its foundations, but that is because that praxis comes from the faith and is a lived expression of it.

4. For the "theologies of liberation" however, the social doctrine of the Church is rejected with disdain. It is said that is comes from the illusion of a possible compromise, typical of the middle class which has no historic destiny.

5. The new *hermeneutic* inherent in the "theologies of liberation" leads to an essentially *political* re-reading of the Scriptures. Thus, a major importance is given to the *Exodus* event inasmuch as it is a liberation from political servitude. Likewise, a political reading of the *Magnificat* is proposed. The mistake here is not in bringing attention to a political dimension of the readings of Scripture, but in making of this one dimension the principal or exclusive component. This leads to a reductionist reading of the Bible.

6. Likewise, one places oneself within the perspective of a temporal messianism, which is one of the most radical of the expressions of secularization of the Kingdom of God and of its absorption into the immanence of human history.

7. In giving such priority to the political dimension, one is led to deny the *radical newness* of the New Testament and above all to misunderstand the person of Our Lord Jesus Christ, true God and true man, and thus the specific character of the salvation he gave us, that is above all liberation from sin, which is the source of all evils.

8. Moreover in setting aside the authoritative interpretation of the Church, denounced as classist, one is at the same time departing from tradition. In that way, one is robbed of an essential theological criterion of interpretation and, in the vacuum

thus created, one welcomes the most radical theses of rationalist exegesis. Without a critical eye, one returns to the opposition of the *"Jesus of history"* versus the *"Jesus of faith"*.

9. Of course the creeds of the faith are literally preserved, especially the Chalcedonian creed, but a new meaning is given to them which is a negation of the faith of the Church. On one hand, the Christological doctrine of Tradition is rejected in the name of class; on the other hand, one claims to meet again the "Jesus of history" coming from the revolutionary experience of the struggle of the poor for their liberation.

10. One claims to be reliving an experience similar to that of Jesus. The experience of the poor struggling for their liberation, which was Jesus' experience, would thus reveal, and it alone, the knowledge of the true God and of the Kingdom.

11. Faith in the Incarnate Word, dead and risen for all men, and whom "God made Lord and Christ" [25] is denied. In its place is substituted a figure of Jesus who is a kind of symbol who sums up in Himself the requirements of the struggle of the oppressed.

12. An exclusively political interpretation is thus given to the death of Christ. In this way, its value for salvation and the whole economy of redemption is denied.

13. This new interpretation thus touches the whole of the Christian mystery.

14. In a general way, this brings about what can be called an inversion of symbols. Thus, instead of seeing, with St. Paul, a figure of Baptism in the Exodus,[26] some end up making of it a symbol of the political liberation of the people.

[25] Cf. *Ac* 2, 36.
[26] Cf. *1 Co* 10, 1-2.

15. When the same hermeneutical criterion is applied to the life and to the hierarchical constitution of the Church, the relationship between the hierarchy and the "base" becomes the relationship of obedient domination to the law of the struggle of the classes. Sacramentality, which is at the root of the ecclesial ministries and which makes of the Church a spiritual reality which cannot be reduced to a purely sociological analysis, is quite simply ignored.

16. This inversion of symbols is likewise verified in the area of the *sacraments*. The Eucharist is no longer to be understood as the real sacramental presence of the reconciling sacrifice, and as the gift of the Body and Blood of Christ. It becomes a celebration of the people in their struggle. As a consequence, the unity of the Church is radically denied. Unity, reconciliation and communion in love are no longer seen as a gift we receive from Christ.[27] It is the historical class of the poor who by means of their struggle will build unity. For them, the struggle of the classes is the way to unity. The Eucharist thus becomes the Eucharist of the class. At the same time, they deny the triumphant force of the love of God which has been given to us.

XI - Orientations

1. The warning against the serious deviations of some "theologies of liberation" must not at all be taken as some kind of approval, even indirect, of those who keep the poor in misery, who profit from that misery, who notice it while doing nothing about it, or who remain indifferent to it. The Church, guided by the Gospel of mercy and by the love for mankind, hears the cry for justice[28] and intends to respond to it with all her might.

[27] Cf. *Ep.* 2, 11-22.
[28] Cf. *Doc. de Puebla,* I, II, 3. 3.

2. Thus a great call goes out to all the Church: with boldness and courage, with farsightedness and prudence, with zeal and strength of spirit, with a love for the poor which demands sacrifice, pastors will consider the response to this call a matter of the highest priority, as many already do.

3. All priests, religious and laypeople who hear this call for justice and who want to work for evangelization and the advancement of mankind, will do so in communion with their bishop and with the Church, each in accord with his or her own specific ecclesial vocation.

4. Aware of the ecclesial character of their vocation, theologians will collaborate loyally and with a spirit of dialogue with the Magisterium of the Church. They will be able to recognize in the Magisterium a gift of Christ to His Church [29] and will welcome its word and its directives with filial respect.

5. It is only when one begins with the task of evangelization understood in its entirety that the authentic requirements of human progress and liberation are appreciated. This liberation has as its indispensable pillars: *the truth about Jesus the Savior, the truth about the Church,* and *the truth about man and his dignity.*[30]

It is in light of the Beatitudes, and especially the Beatitude of the poor of heart, that the Church, which wants to be the Church of the poor throughout the world, intends to come to the aid of the noble struggle for truth and justice. She addresses each person, and for that reason, every person. She is the " universal Church. The Church of the Incarnation. She is not the Church of one class or another. And she speaks in the name of truth itself. This truth is realistic". It leads to a recognition

[29] Cf. *Lk* 10, 16.
[30] Cf. John Paul II, *Address at the Opening of the Conference at Puebla, AAS* 71 (1979) pp. 188-196; *Doc. de Puebla* II P, c. 1.

"of every human reality, every injustice, every tension and every struggle".[31]

6. An effective defense of justice needs to be based on the truth of mankind, created in the image of God and called to the grace of divine sonship. The recognition of the true relationship of human beings to God constitutes the foundation of justice to the extent that it rules the relationships between people. That is why the fight for the rights of man, which the Church does not cease to reaffirm, constitutes the authentic fight for justice.

7. The truth of mankind requires that this battle be fought in ways consistent with human dignity. That is why the systematic and deliberate recourse to blind violence, no matter from which side it comes, must be condemned.[32] To put one's trust in violent means in the hope of restoring more justice is to become the victim of a fatal illusion: violence begets violence and degrades man. It mocks the dignity of man in the person of the victims and it debases that same dignity among those who practice it.

8. The acute need for radical reforms of the structures which conceal poverty and which are themselves forms of violence, should not let us lose sight of the fact that the source of injustice is in the hearts of men. Therefore it is only by making an appeal to the *moral potential* of the person and to the constant need for interior conversion, that social change will be brought about which will truly be in the service of man.[33] For it will only be in the measure that they collaborate freely in these necessary changes through their own initiative and in solidarity, that people, awakened to a sense of their responsibility, will grow in humanity.

[31] Cf. JOHN PAUL II, *Address to the Favela "Vidigal" at Rio de Janeiro,* 2 July 1980, *AAS* 72 (1980) pp. 852-858.

[32] *Doc. de Puebla,* II, c. II, 5. 4.

[33] Cf. *Doc. de Puebla,* IV, c. 3. 3. 1.

The inversion of morality and structures is steeped in a materialist anthropology which is incompatible with the dignity of mankind.

9. It is therefore an equally fatal illusion to believe that these new structures will of themselves give birth to a "new man" in the sense of the truth of man. The Christian cannot forget that it is only the Holy Spirit who has been given to us Who is the source of every true renewal and that God is the Lord of History.

10. By the same token, the overthrow by means of revolutionary violence of structures which generate violence is not *ipso facto* the beginning of a just regime. A major fact of our time ought to evoke the reflection of all those who would sincerely work for the true liberation of their brothers: millions of our own contemporaries legitimately yearn to recover those basic freedoms of which they were deprived by totalitarian and atheistic regimes which came to power by violent and revolutionary means, precisely in the name of the liberation of the people. This shame of our time cannot be ignored: while claiming to bring them freedom, these regimes keep whole nations in conditions of servitude which are unworthy of mankind. Those who, perhaps inadvertently, make themselves accomplices of similar enslavements betray the very poor they mean to help.

11. The class struggle as a road toward a classless society is a myth which slows reform and aggravates poverty and injustice. Those who allow themselves to be caught up in fascination with this myth should reflect on the bitter examples history has to offer about where it leads. They would then understand that we are not talking here about abandoning an effective means of struggle on behalf of the poor for an ideal which has no practical effects. On the contrary, we are talking about freeing oneself from a delusion in order to base oneself squarely on the Gospel and its power of realization.

12. One of the conditions for necessary theological correction is giving proper value to the *social teaching of the Church.* This teaching is by no means closed. It is, on the contrary, open to all the new questions which are so numerous today. In this perspective, the contribution of theologians and other thinkers in all parts of the world to the reflection of the Church is indispensable today.

13. Likewise the experience of those who work directly for evangelization and for the advancement of the poor and the oppressed is necessary for the doctrinal and pastoral reflection of the Church. In this sense, it is necessary to affirm that one becomes more aware of certain aspects of truth by starting with *praxis,* if by that one means pastoral *praxis* and social work which keeps its evangelical inspiration.

14. The teaching of the Church on social issues indicates the main lines of ethical orientation. But in order that it be able to guide action directly, the Church needs competent people from a scientific and technological viewpoint, as well as in the human and political sciences. Pastors should be attentive to the formation of persons of such capability who live the Gospel deeply. Laypersons, whose proper mission is to build society, are involved here to the highest degree.

15. The theses of the "theologies of liberation" are widely popularized under a simplified form, in formation sessions or in what are called "base groups" which lack the necessary catechetical and theological preparation as well as the capacity for discernment. Thus these theses are accepted by generous men and women without any critical judgment being made.

16. That is why pastors must look after the quality and the content of catechesis and formation which should always present the *whole message of salvation* and the imperatives of true liberation within the framework of this whole message.

17. In this full presentation of Christianity, it is proper to emphasize those essential aspects which the "theologies of liberation" especially tend to misunderstand or to eliminate, namely: the transcendance and gratuity of liberation in Jesus Christ, true God and true man; the sovereigny of grace; and the true nature of the means of salvation, especially of the Church and the sacraments. On should also keep in mind the true meaning of ethics in which the distinction between good and evil is not relativized, the real meaning of sin, the necessity for conversion, and the universality of the law of fraternal love.

One needs to be on guard against the politicization of existence which, misunderstanding the entire meaning of the Kingdom of God and the transcendence of the person, begins to sacralize politics and betray the religion of the people in favor of the projects of the revolution.

18. The defenders of orthodoxy are sometimes accused of passivity, indulgence or culpable complicity regarding the intolerable situations of injustice and the political regimes which prolong them. Spiritual conversion, the intensity of the love of God and neighbour, zeal for justice and peace, the Gospel meaning of the poor and of poverty, are required of everyone, and especially of pastors and those in positions of responsibility. The concern for the purity of the faith demands giving the answer of effective witness in the service of one's neighbour, the poor and the oppressed in particular, in an integral theological fashion. By the witness of their dynamic and constructive power to love, Christians will thus lay the foundations of this "civilization of love" of which the Conference of Puebla spoke, following Paul VI.[34] Moreover there are already many priests, religious and laypeople who are consecrated in a truly evangelical way for the creation of a just society.

[34] Cf. *Doc. de Puebla,* IV, II, 2. 3.

Conclusion

The words of Paul VI in his *Profession of Faith,* express with full clarity the faith of the Church, from which one cannot deviate without provoking, besides spiritual disaster, new miseries and new types of slavery.

"We profess our faith that the Kingdom of God, begun here below in the Church of Christ, is not of this world, whose form is passing away, and that its own growth cannot be confused with the progress of civilization, of science of of human technology, but that it consists in knowing ever more deeply the unfathomable riches of Christ, to hope ever more strongly in things eternal, to respond ever more ardently to the love of God, to spread ever more widely grace and holiness among men. But it is this very same love which makes the Church constantly concerned for the true temporal good of mankind as well. Never ceasing to recall to her children that they have no lasting dwelling here on earth, she urges them also to contribute, each according to this own vocation and means, to the welfare of their earthly city, to promote justice, peace and brotherhood among men, to lavish their assistance on their brothers, especially on the poor and the most dispirited. The intense concern of the Church, the bride of Christ, for the needs of mankind, their joys and their hopes, their pains and their struggles, is nothing other than the great desire to be present to them in order to enlighten them with the light of Christ, and join them all to Him, their only Savior. It can never mean that the Church is conforming to the things of this world, nor that she is lessening the earnestness with which she awaits her Lord and the eternal Kingdom".[35]

[35] Paul VI, *Profession of Faith of the People of God,* 30 June 1968, *AAS* 60 (1968) pp. 443-444.

This Instruction was adopted at an Ordinary Meeting of the Sacred Congregation for the Doctrine of the Faith and was approved at an audience granted to the undersigned Cardinal Prefect by His Holiness Pope John Paul II, who ordered its publication.

Given at Rome, at the Sacred Congregation for the Doctrine of the Faith, on August 6, 1984, the Feast of the Transfiguration of Our Lord.

JOSEPH Card. RATZINGER
Prefect

✠ ALBERTO BOVONE
Titular Archbishop of Caesarea in Numidia
Secretary